To the Moon and E

T0364521

The Story of Katherine Johnson

Contents

Written by Sandra Agard

Illustrated by Amanda Quartey

Collins

Who was Katherine Johnson?

You've probably heard of Neil Armstrong, the first man to walk on the Moon. But did you know that he may never have got there without the help of one woman?

Katherine Johnson was a mathematician. She used maths to help people get to outer space and even to the Moon.

Although she never left Earth, her path to working with rockets at the American Space Agency was just as difficult as a journey to the stars.

Katherine faced many challenges. She was an African-American woman living at a time when the USA had many laws stopping Black people getting certain jobs and living in certain places. She had to fight against **racism** *and* **sexism**.

This book begins when she was a young girl – a young girl who loved numbers.

1 Katherine loves numbers

Katherine was born in White Sulphur Springs, West Virginia, USA, on 26th August 1918.

Her parents were Joylette and Joshua Coleman. Her mother was a teacher and her father was a farmer, builder and handyman who worked at the famous Greenbrier Hotel.

Katherine was the youngest of four children. From an early age, Katherine loved numbers and was eager to learn. She saw numbers, patterns and shapes everywhere and would count everything. When she was at home, she'd count the plates on the table.

When she went outside, she'd count the trees and at night, she'd count the stars in the sky.

By the age of four, Katherine could spell many words and knew her multiplication tables. One day she followed her brother, Charlie, to school and stayed with him all day, helping him to solve maths problems in class.

The teacher, Mrs Leftwich, was so astonished, she went to see Katherine's mother. It was decided that Katherine should start school in the autumn when she was aged just four. This was unusual in the USA, where children normally start school aged between five and six.

When the term began, Katherine went to school with her brothers and sister. Because she knew her numbers and could read and write well, teachers felt she should skip three grades and put her in the second grade, with children aged seven years.

As well as numbers, Katherine loved to read and would often go to the library.

Fact box

Black children and White children were educated separately up until 1954, owing to US **segregation**.

2 School days

In September 1926, Mr and Mrs Coleman made a decision that would change the family's lives forever. They decided to leave their home in White Sulphur so the children could attend the West Virginia Colored Institute, as there were no high schools for children in their home town.

Fact box

The West Virginia Colored Institute was built in 1891. It educated Black children and also offered teacher training.

Unable to find work near the Institute, Mr Coleman returned to White Sulphur Springs. For the next eight years, he only saw his family during the holidays and in the summer when he travelled back to see them. During this time, all four children completed high school and four-year university programmes.

Katherine attended the elementary school on
the institute's grounds. She was a fast learner and
her potential in mathematics was quickly discovered.
She went from middle school to high school aged ten and
was surrounded by children who were 14 and 15 years old.

Even though Katherine was busy at school, her mother got her to do jobs around the house. She would be given books to read, and she was taught to sew, cook and play the piano.

Katherine also liked to play with her brothers, so she learnt to play tennis. Later, her brothers taught her how to ride a motorbike and drive a car. Women at this time did not usually learn such things. As well as this, Black women were not expected to have such knowledge.

Katherine was always looking for new achievements and wanted to do extra work after school. When she was 13 one of her teachers, Professor Evans, became the Head of the Maths Department. He asked her to do some office work, including filing and typing. However, he soon discovered she couldn't type, so when the family went back to White Sulphur for the summer holidays, he gave Katherine a typewriter, paper and a typing book. He expected her to be able to type on her return to school in the autumn. She did learn, through lots of practice, and this was to prove vital for her later career.

Katherine graduated from high school in West Virginia in the spring of 1932 aged 14, five years early. When she returned after the summer, she started her university education aged just 14.

Learning to type during the summer proved extremely fortunate as Katherine managed to get a job in the office of President Davis, the university principal. This helped her to pay for the cost of university. Katherine got to know all the professors, including Dr Claytor, a professor of mathematics.

Katherine graduating from high school

Katherine originally planned to study French at university. However, Dr Claytor had other ideas. He saw Katherine's potential to be a great mathematician and wanted her to study mathematics. In the end, she decided to study both subjects. She even took extra maths classes.

It was Dr Claytor who first told her about becoming a research mathematician. This was a job that involved solving problems using maths. Katherine loved solving problems and wanted to know more.

Dr Claytor

As part of the maths course, Dr Claytor developed classes in **geometry** of outer space, just for Katherine.

In 1937 aged 18, Katherine graduated from West Virginia State College with degrees in mathematics and French and the highest marks of any student in the institute's 46-year history.

Katherine graduating from university

3 Becoming a teacher

Katherine dreamt of becoming a teacher, like her mother.
She got her first teaching job after graduation. Still just
18, she began working at Carnegie Elementary School
in Marion, Virginia. She taught maths, French and
music, passing on her love of these subjects to
the teenage students.

In maths, Katherine taught her students all the things that
make up mathematics. She taught them how to use rulers,
compasses, protractors, decimal points and fractions.
She wanted her students to understand the background of
what they were working out and urged them to be curious.
Katherine said, "If you lose your curiosity, then you
stop learning."

During the first term at school, Katherine was asked to put on a play as a fundraiser for the school.

She was going to play the piano, but they needed a male singer, and she was introduced to Jimmie Goble, a fellow teacher. They soon discovered they had a lot in common, becoming friends. Not long afterwards Jimmie asked Katherine to marry him.

They married on 9th November 1939, but had to keep their marriage secret as the law at the time did not allow married women to teach in the classroom.

In the spring of 1940, Katherine wanted to continue her studies but there were no **postgraduate** courses available for Black students. Times were changing, though, and laws were being passed forcing White institutions to change their policies.

One day, the president of West Virginia University, the state's all-White college, Dr Lawall, visited President Davis, the president of Katherine's former college. Dr Lawall wanted to award places to three exceptional Black students in the university graduate programme. President Davis was happy with this proposal as he saw it as an opportunity for his African-American students to work in better-resourced facilities.

Katherine was asked to be one of the students. She was extremely excited and left teaching at the high school to enrol in the summer graduate programme at West Virginia University.

The only difficulty she had was finding a course that she hadn't already covered. Her professors at West Virginia State Institute had prepared her well.

After the programme ended, Katherine didn't return to teaching as she was expecting a baby. Katherine became a full-time mother and, eventually, she and Jimmie had three daughters: Joylette, Connie and Kathy.

In 1944, Katherine returned to teaching in the local Black high school.

Katherine and her daughters

In 1949, two tragedies struck Katherine's family. First, a fire destroyed their home, forcing them to return to White Sulphur Springs to live with Katherine's parents. Then her brother Horace became ill and sadly passed away.

Life was soon to change again when Katherine heard about exciting new job opportunities at Langley Air Force Base. In the 1950s, the US government's department – National Advisory Committee on Aeronautics (NACA) – began hiring hundreds of new employees, including mathematicians. Katherine applied; the pay was much better than her current job and, more importantly, it was a chance to use the maths she had studied to tackle exciting new challenges.

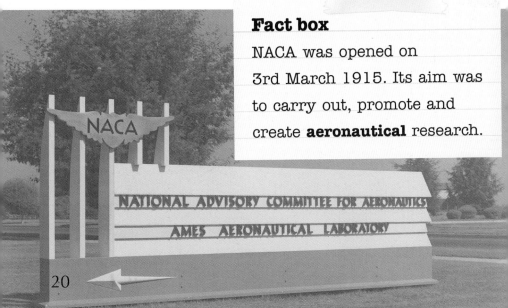

Fact box

NACA was opened on 3rd March 1915. Its aim was to carry out, promote and create **aeronautical** research.

4 Becoming a human computer

Katherine started work in June 1953, as a human computer or a "computer in a skirt" as the women were called, at NACA, Langley Research Center, Virginia. The women should have been called mathematicians. They worked on complicated mathematical problems to enable aeroplanes to fly and map their flight paths.

At Langley, Katherine met Dorothy Vaughan and Mary Jackson. Dorothy Vaughan was a mathematician and managed the section where Katherine worked. She would become the first African-American supervisor at Langley. Mary Jackson was also a mathematician and became NACA's first Black aerospace **engineer**. She also helped other Black women get hired and promoted in the field of engineering. These three women would become lifelong friends and support each other throughout their careers.

Dorothy Vaughan

Mary Jackson

At first, Katherine worked on wind tunnel experiments. Wind tunnels are large tubes with air blowing through them and are used to learn more about how an aeroplane will fly.

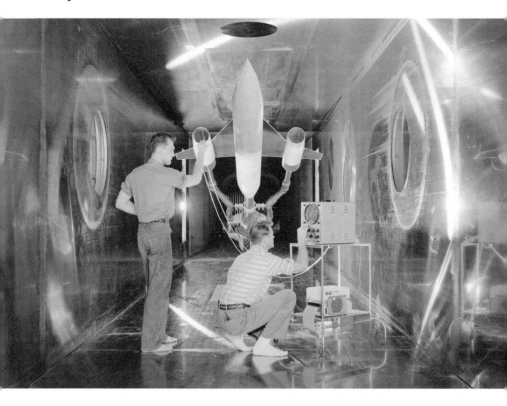

One day, Dorothy Vaughan told Katherine about an opportunity in another department. The Flight Research Division needed two new human computers. This department specialised in testing real planes flying through the sky instead of using wind tunnels.

In her new department, the Flight Research Division, Katherine was ignored by her White male colleagues.

When she arrived in the office and sat at a desk, the man sitting next to her got up and moved away without a word. He didn't want to work with a Black woman.

Katherine and her colleague Erma Tynes Walker, who was also a Black woman, always acted professionally and politely. They soon gained the respect of their new colleagues by doing their jobs to an exceptionally high standard.

Dorothy organised for Katherine to become a permanent member of the Flight Research Division and the new team soon saw the potential of Katherine's mathematical skills.

In this department, she worked with engineers to discover how aeroplanes could travel faster than the speed of sound and if they'd be able to fly in outer space.

Fact box

The speed of sound is how quickly sound waves travel through the air. This is approximately 343 metres per second. It is affected by air temperature and the material that the sound is travelling through.

As she had done all her life, Katherine began to ask a lot of questions. She was eager to learn and very curious. The engineers in the division taught her many things about flight and space travel that would prove vital during Katherine's career.

Katherine's first job was to find the cause of an aeroplane crash. A small plane had dropped out of the sky for no apparent reason.

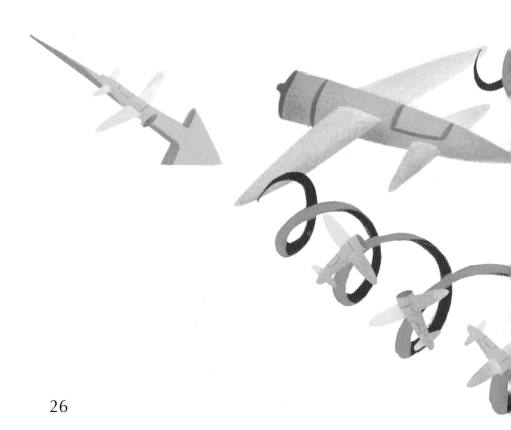

Katherine studied the data and photographs to work out why the plane crashed. She worked out that large planes disturb the air in a similar way to a ship moving through water, leaving waves behind it. Flying through this path of disturbed air can cause small planes to break down and crash.

As a result of her discovery, new air traffic rules were created. Minimum distances were now required between flight paths to prevent future accidents. This made flying much safer. Katherine had shown that a woman could do research just as well as a man, and she became the first woman to have her name on such reports.

5 The Space Race begins

In the late 1950s, the USA and the **USSR** began competing over who had the best space technology. They wanted to see who could get to space first. This was known as the Space Race.

On 4th October 1957, the USSR launched the **satellite**, *Sputnik*. It was the first artificial satellite to orbit, or go round, Earth. The Space Race had begun, and the Americans were losing.

Fact box

"Sputnik" is **Russian** for traveller.

In response to the USSR's success, in 1958, NACA became NASA (National Aeronautics and Space Administration). This was a clear sign that space exploration was now a priority for the USA. Their aim was to become the first country to put a man in space, but they were beaten by the USSR, again.

On 12th April 1961, the Russian **cosmonaut** Yuri Gagarin became the first man to orbit Earth.

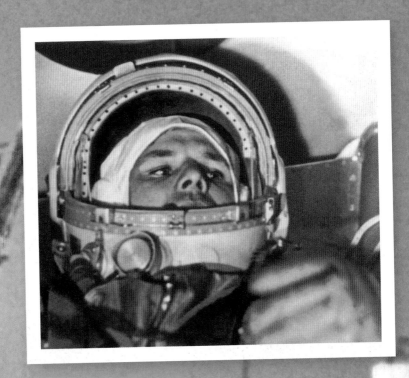

During this time, Katherine saw major changes in her workplace. At the start of 1957, the human computers were beginning to be replaced by electronic ones.

Langley Research Center, where Katherine worked, had purchased its first "electronic calculator" in 1947. It had a clear advantage over the human computers. It performed the same work as the women but much faster and it could work throughout the night, whereas human computers had to rest.

Supersonic flights were becoming more difficult to calculate. The maths needed for the calculations could take up to a month to work out. The human computers were seen to be too slow to work out the maths problems.

However, the electronic computers had their problems too. They were huge, occupied entire rooms and were noisy and disruptive. Whole buildings would shake as they churned out data.

Plus, they made mistakes. Despite these issues, the use of electronic computers continued to increase because of their speed.

As the electronic computers began replacing human computers, Dorothy Vaughan came up with a plan to make sure that she and other women in her department kept their jobs. The electronic computers needed to be programmed – a human needed to tell them what to calculate and how to calculate it. Dorothy taught herself and many women in her department how to do this so that they'd still be needed, even after the electronic computers replaced their jobs.

Katherine remained invaluable during this period. In fact, her maths skills were so respected that her bosses would get her to check if the electronic computers had made any mistakes. She was still more accurate than the new machines.

Katherine was keen to help with the Space Race. However, despite being respected for her abilities, she still faced challenges. The male scientists and engineers did not like working with women. They made it difficult for women to attend the editorial meetings where the decisions on space flight were being made. Katherine began to question why she couldn't be included, as she was doing the mathematical calculations.

Men gave the orders, and women took the notes. Women had to prove that they could do the work as well as any man. Katherine thought this wrong, and unfair. She wanted to go to the editorial meetings as this was where the important decisions were made.

Katherine kept asking to be permitted into the editorial meetings until the men in charge, tired of her persistence, finally allowed her to attend.

In 1958, Katherine officially joined the team in charge of those editorial meetings, the Guidance and Control Branch of Langley's Flight Research Division. She was eager to learn and had a lot of knowledge to pass on.

6 Reaching for the stars

In 1958, Katherine met the man who would become her second husband, James Johnson. Her first husband Jimmie had passed away in 1956.

James Johnson was an army captain. During the Second World War, he had become an expert on aircraft maintenance and repair. Katherine and James both loved aeroplanes.

James Johnson, Katherine Johnson's second husband

Back at Langley, Katherine and the research team were now working fully on the space program. They had to work fast, for world events were moving quickly and everybody was under pressure.

One major difficulty holding back the US team was working out how to bring a rocket back to Earth safely. They couldn't risk sending men into space until they had made sure that the rocket could land safely in the ocean. The rocket would travel in a massive curve, known as parabola, that looks like an upside-down U. By working out this path, they could ensure the rocket would land where they wanted it to. This is where Katherine stepped in.

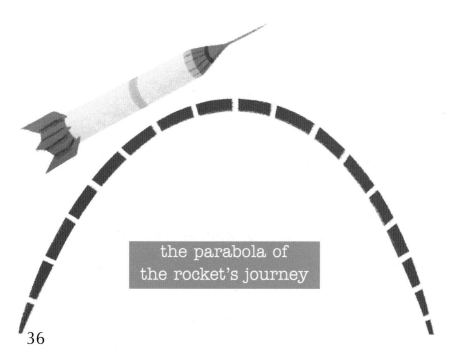

the parabola of
the rocket's journey

She worked out the path the rocket would take based on how high it was flying, how fast it was going and when it would take off. Using this information, NASA was confident that the rocket would land safely.

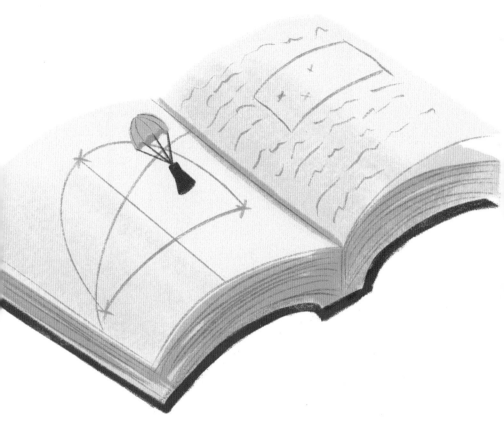

The agency was reluctant to use electronic calculators for such dangerous missions. So, Katherine's mathematical skills and accuracy were essential during this time. She checked everything manually.

Katherine always said that women were capable of doing anything men could do and now she had proven it by solving this incredibly complex problem.

On 5th May 1961, Alan Shepard blasted off in the rocket named *Freedom 7*. It was a successful launch and the rocket soared into space, kilometres above Earth. The flight lasted 15 minutes.

Katherine worked out the exact point where *Freedom 7* would touch down in the Atlantic Ocean.

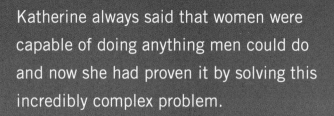

the rocket *Freedom 7*

Freedom 7 returned safely. Katherine's long hours of working on the maths and calculating the data had been worth it.

Now the USA wanted to go into space again, but for a longer flight. This time the mission was to orbit Earth and, once again, Katherine would play an important role.

Alan Shepard safely landed back on Earth

The name of the rocket was *Friendship 7*, and the astronaut was John Glenn. Calculations for this space trip were done by the electronic computers. However, John refused to go on the mission if Katherine was not allowed to work on the calculations. He trusted her judgement more than he trusted the machines.

Katherine was determined to work out the right numbers for the flight's pathways. She worked tirelessly to get everything right. She checked all the numbers countless times and didn't use the electronic computers. It took her a day and a half to work out the calculations – the same time it took the machines. There could be no room for errors.

On 20th February, 1962, astronaut John Glenn became the first American astronaut to orbit Earth. The takeoff went without any problems.

John Glenn entering Friendship 7

However, during the first of three orbits, a problem occurred. The automatic control system failed, so Glenn had to manually operate the rocket. During the second orbit, the heat shield came loose. This was potentially dangerous. On re-entering Earth's atmosphere, Glenn would be exposed to temperatures as high as 3000 degrees. NASA got Glenn to make some adjustments and he landed safely.

heat shield

Katherine, like the rest of America, watched on her television as *Friendship 7* re-entered Earth's atmosphere.

Landing *Friendship 7* in the Atlantic Ocean near the Bahamas, John Glenn emerged from the capsule to great praise.

Katherine Johnson and the team had done a remarkable job.

7 To the Moon and back

Following the success of flights *Freedom 7* and *Friendship 7*, the USA now wanted to send astronauts to the Moon. This would be ground-breaking but also difficult and dangerous. Katherine and the engineers would have to work extremely hard to make this another successful mission.

The USSR had the same idea. They had been the first to achieve every major milestone in space so far. They wanted to continue being first. The USA wanted to finally beat the USSR in the Space Race.

Katherine began work on a project called Apollo 11, which aimed to launch men into space in a rocket called *Saturn V* and land on the Moon.

The USA's President Kennedy visiting NASA, 23 February 1962

Right from the beginning, it was decided that the new electronic computers would be used to do the calculations. They worked much faster than people and their accuracy had massively improved.

The astronauts chosen for this mission were Neil Armstrong, Buzz Aldrin and Michael Collins, and they would go on to make history.

NASA were planning something new for this trip to the Moon. The mission would use a vehicle called a Lunar Lander that transported the astronauts on the Moon's surface. They called it *The Eagle*.

Neil Armstrong, Michael Collins and Buzz Aldrin

The launch of *Saturn V* took place at the Kennedy Center in Florida on 16th July, 1969. The journey took over three days and on 20th July the rocket landed on the Moon.

Katherine made every mission possible as she always checked the computers' numbers manually and was known for her accuracy. She was trusted even more than the computers. Her calculations were essential in linking up the command centre in Florida with *The Eagle* and helped the astronauts return home safely.

8 Katherine Johnson's legacy

Katherine Johnson worked at NASA for 33 years. During that time, her calculations proved crucial to countless missions into space and many were used in future missions. She even did calculations for future planned missions to Mars. She wrote 26 research reports and taught countless students during her career.

The impact Katherine had on space travel is undeniable but, for many years after her retirement in 1986, her story went unknown.

Katherine Johnson receives the Equal Opportunity Award, 4th February, 1985 at NASA Langley Research Center.

49

Katherine began getting recognition when, in 1999, she was named West Virginia State College Outstanding Alumnus of the Year. In 2015 she received the Presidential Medal of Freedom from President Obama.

In 2017, NASA opened the Katherine G Johnson building at the Langley Research Center, the place where her successful career began 64 years earlier. She received many other awards, but her most prized possession was an American flag that had flown to the Moon and back.

Katherine receiving the Presidential Medal of Freedom

Katherine loved space and wanted others to share her passion. She created textbooks and urged students to ask questions and follow their dreams. She was a true trailblazer and paved the way for others to follow.

Katherine Johnson passed away aged 101 on 24th February 2020. She went from being a young girl who loved numbers to a woman whose love of maths changed the world. Her life will continue to inspire us all to the Moon and back.

Glossary

aeronautical the science or practice of building or flying aircraft

cosmonaut the Russian (USSR) word for astronaut

engineer someone who designs, builds, tests or maintains engines, machines or structures

geometry type of mathematics that looks at shapes and figures; used in building houses and bridges and to plan space travel

postgraduate a student who has completed an undergraduate course at university or college

racism unfair treatment based on race/colour of skin

Russian from the USSR

satellite a spacecraft that is sent into orbit around a planet or star to send back information

segregation separating people according to characteristics such as race or gender

sexism prejudice, discrimination and stereotyping against one gender

Sputnik three Earth satellites launched by the USSR; the first satellite was launched on 4th October 1957

supersonic the act of exceeding the speed of sound waves through air

USSR the Union of Soviet Socialist Republics that spread in Europe and Asia; it existed from 1922 to 1991

Index

Timeline

26th August 1918: Katherine Johnson born

1925

1st May 1932: graduates from high school

1935

1953: begins work as a computer at NACA's Langley Research Center

1945

1955

1962: John Glenn becomes the first American to orbit Earth after his spacecraft follows the flight path confirmed by Katherine

1965

1975

1986: retires from NASA

1985

1995

2015: awarded the Presidential Medal of Freedom

2005

2017: NASA opens The Katherine G. Johnson Computational Research Facility

2015

2025

1937: graduates from college with a Bachelor of Science in mathematics and French

1961: calculates the flight path for Alan Shepard's *Freedom 7*, making him the first American in space

1969: *Apollo 11* is the first manned mission to land on the Moon; Katherine was part of the team that made this possible

24th February 2020: dies aged 101

1920
1930
1940
1950
1960
1970
1980
1990
2000
2010
2020

Ideas for reading

Written by Gill Matthews
Primary Literacy Consultant

Reading objectives:
- check that the book makes sense to them, discussing their understanding and exploring the meaning of words in context
- retrieve, record and present information from non-fiction
- explain and discuss their understanding of what they have read, including through formal presentations and debates, maintaining a focus on the topic and using notes where necessary
- provide reasoned justifications for their views.

Spoken language objectives:
- articulate and justify answers, arguments and opinions
- participate in discussions, presentations, performances, role play, improvisations and debates

Curriculum links: Science – Earth and Space

Interest words: legacy, successful, passion, trailblazer, inspire

Resources: IT

Build a context for reading

- Ask children to look at the front cover and suggest what they think the book might be about.
- Read the back-cover blurb. Discuss why the children think Katherine Johnson had to fight agains racism and sexism.
- Point out that this is a biography. Check what children know about biographies. Ask what features they think it will have.
- Give children time to skim the book to find the contents, glossary and index.

Understand and apply reading strategies

- Read pp4–6 aloud. Ask children what they have heard that they found particularly interesting and/or surprising. Encourage them to support their responses with reasons.
- Ask children to read pp7–14. Discuss what kind of person they think Katherine Johnson was. Explore what it might have been like for her to be at school with children four or five years older than her.